EXPLORING THE STATES

Illinois

THE PRAIRIE STATE

by Amy Rechner

BELLWETHER MEDIA • MINNEAPOLIS, MN

Note to Librarians, Teachers, and Parents:

Blastoff! Readers are carefully developed by literacy experts and combine standards-based content with developmentally appropriate text.

Level 1 provides the most support through repetition of high-frequency words, light text, predictable sentence patterns, and strong visual support.

Level 2 offers early readers a bit more challenge through varied simple sentences, increased text load, and less repetition of high-frequency words.

Level 3 advances early-fluent readers toward fluency through increased text and concept load, less reliance on visuals, longer sentences, and more literary language.

Level 4 builds reading stamina by providing more text per page, increased use of punctuation, greater variation in sentence patterns, and increasingly challenging vocabulary.

Level 5 encourages children to move from "learning to read" to "reading to learn" by providing even more text, varied writing styles, and less familiar topics.

Whichever book is right for your reader, Blastoff! Readers are the perfect books to build confidence and encourage a love of reading that will last a lifetime!

This edition first published in 2014 by Bellwether Media, Inc.

No part of this publication may be reproduced in whole or in part without written permission of the publisher. For information regarding permission, write to Bellwether Media, Inc., Attention: Permissions Department, 5357 Penn Avenue South, Minneapolis, MN 55419.

Library of Congress Cataloging-in-Publication Data

Rechner, Amy.
 Illinois / by Amy Rechner.
   pages cm. – (Blastoff! readers. Exploring the states)
 Includes bibliographical references and index.
 Summary: "Developed by literacy experts for students in grades three through seven, this book introduces young readers to the geography and culture of Illinois"–Provided by publisher.
 ISBN 978-1-62617-012-4 (hardcover : alk. paper)
 1. Illinois–Juvenile literature. I. Title.
 F541.3.R44 2014
 977.3–dc23

                                                              2013002387

Printed in the United States of America, North Mankato, MN.

Table of Contents

Where Is Illinois?

Illinois is a narrow state in the heart of the **Midwest**. It covers 57,916 square miles (150,002 square kilometers). Wisconsin lies to the north. The Mississippi River separates Illinois from Iowa and Missouri to the west. Indiana lies to the east. In the southeast, the Ohio River separates Illinois and Kentucky.

The southern tip of Lake Michigan forms Illinois' northeastern border. Chicago, the nation's third-largest city, lies along Lake Michigan's shore. The state capital of Springfield is in the middle of the state.

Wisconsin

Lake
Michigan

Rockford

Chicago

Iowa

Starved Rock
State Park

Indiana

Illinois

★ **Springfield**

Missouri

Mississippi River

N
W E
S

Kentucky

History

People first arrived in Illinois around 10,000 years ago. They hunted animals and gathered wild plants for food. **Native** peoples later grew corn on the **prairie**. French explorers arrived in 1673. Other European settlers soon followed. They built factories, farms, and towns. Illinois became a state in 1818. Chicago grew from a tiny trading post to a huge city.

Chicago in 1820

Illinois Timeline!

1673: French explorers Louis Jolliet and Jacques Marquette are the first Europeans to visit the region.

1763: France loses Illinois to Britain after the French and Indian War.

1818: Illinois becomes the twenty-first state.

1832: Native American warrior Black Hawk leads two tribes in a fight for their land. The U.S. government wins the Black Hawk War, and the tribes move out of Illinois.

1860: Springfield lawyer Abraham Lincoln is elected the sixteenth President of the United States.

1871: The Great Chicago Fire burns for two days. Downtown Chicago is almost completely destroyed.

1980: Illinois native Ronald Reagan is elected the fortieth U.S. President.

2008: Illinois senator Barack Obama is elected the forty-fourth President of the United States.

Black Hawk

Abraham Lincoln

Barack Obama

The Land

Illinois is nicknamed the Prairie State for a good reason. Most of the state is a flat **plain** that was once covered in prairie grass. The grasses made the soil rich and perfect for farming. Illinois is so long that its north and south have different climates. Northern Illinois has cold winters with a lot of snow. The south is much warmer.

Canals connect rivers across Illinois. The canals create a shipping route from the **Great Lakes** to the Mississippi River. Many of the state's lakes are also human-made. The largest ones were built as **reservoirs** to store water for later use.

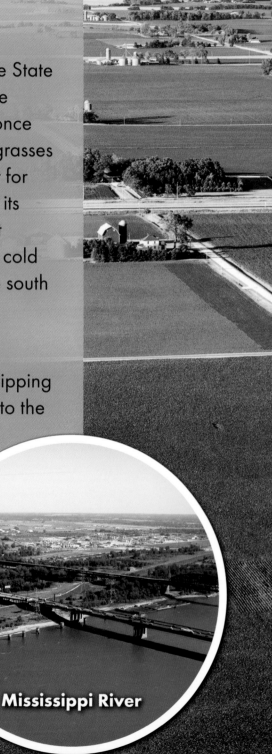

Mississippi River

Illinois' Climate

average °F

spring
Low: 39°
High: 60°

summer
Low: 62°
High: 83°

fall
Low: 42°
High: 63°

winter
Low: 18°
High: 34°

Starved Rock State Park

Starved Rock State Park is a welcome break in the flat land of Illinois. Its towering sandstone **bluffs** line the Illinois River. Steep sandstone cliffs stand out next to the forested bluffs. The bluffs are split by a string of eighteen **canyons**. The canyons were formed by melting **glaciers** and streams.

Each canyon has a waterfall. Some are bigger than others. The waterfalls are especially powerful in spring, when melting snow and rain bring a rush of water. Miles of hiking trails wind through the woods and connect the canyons. Bald eagles are sometimes spotted fishing for their food.

Starved Rock Peak

fun fact

Starved Rock State Park got its name from a battle between Native American tribes. A group of Illiniwek starved to death after their foes trapped them on top of a tall rock.

Wildlife

The prairies and forests of Illinois support all kinds of wildlife. White-tailed deer and foxes live in wooded areas. Coyotes and raccoons roam countryside and cities in search of food. Rivers provide homes for muskrats, beavers, and fish such as bass and carp.

The Shawnee National Forest and the state's river valleys attract a variety of birds. **Migratory** birds come in the spring and leave in the fall. Owls and hawks stay through the winter. Tall grasses and wildflowers fill the Illinois prairie. Goldenrods, asters, and violets color fields in shades of purple and gold.

white-tailed deer

great horned owl

fox

coyote

Landmarks

Chicago's Navy **Pier** is a big Illinois attraction. Shops, restaurants, and other amusements fill this walkway on the shore of Lake Michigan. Cahokia **Mounds** State Historic Site is in southwestern Illinois. It was the home of an ancient community. The site preserves 68 of the more than 120 mounds that they built. The Garden of the Gods is a collection of natural sandstone formations in the Shawnee National Forest. Hiking trails wind through the peaks and cliffs.

Fans of Abraham Lincoln flock to Springfield. Tours of his home, law offices, and Presidential Library and Museum bring his world to life. West of Springfield is New Salem. The small village has been restored to look as it did when young Lincoln lived there.

Cahokia Mounds

Lincoln's house

Navy Pier

Chicago

fun fact

The world's first skyscraper was built in Chicago in 1885.

Chicago is famous for its **diversity**. People come from around the world to live and work there. In downtown Chicago, Millennium Park features sculptures and fountains that people can interact with for fun. The Old Water Tower and Pumping Station stand on Michigan Avenue. They survived the Great Chicago Fire.

Willis Tower

Millennium Park

Willis Tower is the tallest building in North America. Amazing views await those who ride up to the Skydeck on the 103rd floor. Visitors to Chicago also enjoy shops, museums, an aquarium, and a free zoo. Dozens of theaters show plays, concerts, and dance performances. Everyone delights in the parks and beaches along Lake Michigan.

Working

fun fact

Illinois is a sweet place to live! Tootsie Rolls, Lemonheads, Oreos, and other famous treats are made in factories there.

Illinois is one of the top farming states in the country. Miles of farmland stretch across the state for as far as the eye can see. The main crops are corn and soybeans. Farmers also raise cows and pigs. Products from Illinois farms are used to make paint, makeup products, and other goods.

Illinois factories also produce machinery, chemicals, food products, and fuels. Coal, oil, and limestone are mined throughout the state. These goods and resources are shipped over the state's roads, railways, and waterways. Many people in cities have **service jobs**. They work in banks, office buildings, and hospitals.

Where People Work in Illinois

government
12%

farming and
natural resources
1%

manufacturing
9%

services
78%

Playing

Illinois may be flat, but it isn't dull. Boaters and fishers enjoy its many lakes and rivers. Hikers and campers explore the state parks. Cold winters invite Illinoisans to go ice fishing and cross-country skiing. Music concerts and theater productions keep people in cities entertained all year.

Illinois is also a great state for sports fans. Chicago has a team in every professional sport. Baseball fans are split between two teams. They root for the Cubs or the White Sox. True Chicago fans never cheer for both!

fun fact

The Chicago Cubs have not competed in the World Series since 1945. Many fans believe the team was cursed by a man who was asked to leave Wrigley Field because his pet goat was smelly.

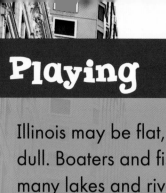

Horseshoe Sandwich

Ingredients:

1 (9 ounce) bag frozen french fries
1 pound ground beef
4 slices bread, toasted

cheese sauce:
Each restaurant has their own!
To make a pre-made sauce
special, add seasonings
like salt, pepper, hot sauce,
or Worcestershire sauce until
it is the perfect combination.

Directions:

1. Preheat the oven to
   400°F. Bake french
   fries on a baking sheet for
   20 minutes, or until golden brown.

2. Divide the ground beef into four equal parts and
   form into patties.

3. Fry the patties in a large skillet over medium-high
   heat until well done, about 4 minutes per side.

4. Place a slice of toasted bread on each of 4 dinner
   plates. Top each slice with a hamburger patty.
   Place cooked french fries on top of each patty.

5. Pour cheese sauce on top. Serve immediately.

   Makes 4 sandwiches.

Chicago hot dog

deep-dish pizza

Visitors to Illinois should bring an appetite. Chicago is famous for all-beef hot dogs, Italian beef sandwiches, and deep-dish pizza. It is also a great place to try food from other cultures, such as Indian or Middle Eastern dishes. Each year, the Taste of Chicago food festival offers samples from dozens of area restaurants.

Springfield is the home of the horseshoe sandwich. This is a giant open-faced ham or beef sandwich topped with french fries and cheese sauce. Barbecue ribs are popular all over the state. Popcorn is the official snack food of Illinois.

Festivals

Illinois has fun when the weather is warm and the days are long. The Chicago summer is filled with art shows and all kinds of music festivals. In August, the Air and Water Show zooms into Chicago. Lisle hosts the Eyes to the Skies Festival in July. More than a dozen hot air balloons crowd the sky and glow at dusk.

The Illinois State Fair in Springfield celebrates the state's farm products and livestock. People from across the state enjoy the music, displays, and food. Fair specialties include deep-fried brownies and corn dogs.

Illinois State Fair

Air and Water Show

Funny Business

Chicago Theatre

Illinois has a long history of comedy. Charlie Chaplin made a silent movie in Chicago in 1915. The Marx Brothers tried farming in Illinois before they became a famous comedy team. Chicagoan Harold Ramis co-wrote the comedies *Ghostbusters* and *Caddyshack*. Bill Murray, a star in both movies, is from Wilmette. *Ferris Bueller's Day Off* and *Home Alone* were filmed around Chicago.

Richard Pryor

Melissa McCarthy

Jane Lynch

Many comedians on television today trained at Chicago's Second City comedy club. Actors at Second City perform comedy **sketches**, like the Marx Brothers did. They also learn how to **improvise** funny skits. Comedy combines hard work with fun. Working hard and having fun is what Illinois is all about!

Fast Facts About Illinois

ILLINOIS

Illinois' Flag

Illinois' flag is white with the state seal in the center. The seal shows an eagle carrying a shield with 13 stars and 13 stripes. They represent the original colonies. In the eagle's mouth is a banner with the state motto, "State Sovereignty, National Union." A carved rock shows the dates of statehood and the adoption of the state seal.

State Flower
violet

State Nicknames:	The Prairie State The Land of Lincoln
State Motto:	"State Sovereignty, National Union"
Year of Statehood:	1818
Capital City:	Springfield
Other Major Cities:	Chicago, Aurora, Rockford
Population:	12,830,632 (2010)
Area:	57,916 square miles (150,002 square kilometers); Illinois is the 25th largest state.
Major Industries:	farming, manufacturing, mining
Natural Resources:	coal, lumber, water, soil
State Government:	118 representatives; 59 senators
Federal Government:	18 representatives; 2 senators
Electoral Votes:	20

State Bird
northern cardinal

State Animal
white-tailed deer

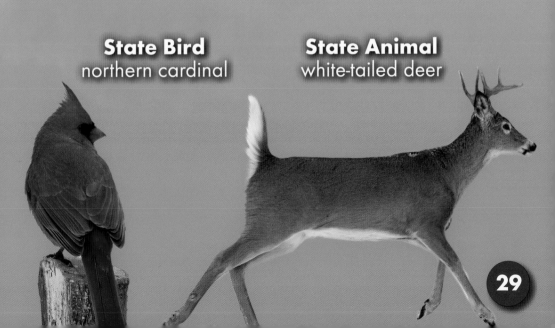

29

Glossary

bluffs—cliffs or steep banks

canals—waterways that are usually built to connect larger bodies of water

canyons—deep valleys with steep sides

diversity—variety of people from many different backgrounds

glaciers—massive sheets of ice that cover large areas of land

Great Lakes—five large freshwater lakes on the border between the United States and Canada

improvise—to make up without preparation

Midwest—a region of 12 states in the north-central United States

migratory—traveling from one place to another, often with the seasons

mounds—small hills built by humans; mounds are sometimes created to mark graves.

native—originally from a specific place

pier—a walkway that extends into a body of water

plain—a large area of flat land

prairie—a large area of level or rolling grassland

reservoirs—places where water is collected and stored for use

service jobs—jobs that perform tasks for people or businesses

sketches—short comedy pieces

To Learn More

AT THE LIBRARY

Burgan, Michael. *Illinois*. New York, N.Y.: Children's Press, 2008.

Cleland, Joann. *Surviving the Great Chicago Fire*. Vero Beach, Fla.: Rourke Pub., 2010.

Smith, Rich. *Illinois*. Edina, Minn.: ABDO Pub. Co., 2010.

ON THE WEB

Learning more about Illinois is as easy as 1, 2, 3.

1. Go to www.factsurfer.com.

2. Enter "Illinois" into the search box.

3. Click the "Surf" button and you will see a list of related Web sites.

With factsurfer.com, finding more information is just a click away.

Index

The images in this book are reproduced through the courtesy of: Songquan Deng, front cover, pp. 14-15; (Collection)/ Prints & Photographs Division/ Library of Congress, pp. 6, 7 (left, middle, right); Blackie, p. 8 (small); Steve Geer, pp. 8-9; Jason Patrick Ross, pp. 10-11; Chuck Eckert/ Alamy, p. 11 (small); Denis Pepin, pp. 12-13; Pim Leijen, p. 12 (left); Amst, p. 12 (middle); James Marvin Phelps, p. 12 (right); Ira Block/ National Geographic/ SuperStock, p. 14 (left); Nagel Phtography, p. 14 (right); Visions of America/ SuperStock, pp. 16-17; Gary718, p. 17 (small); Bloomberg/ Getty Images, p. 18; Scott Olson/ Getty Images, p. 19; Andrey Bayda, pp. 20-21; Ron Vesely/ Getty Images, p. 20 (small); Jon Eppard, p. 22; Lauri Patterson, p. 23; Shinyshot, p. 23 (small); Maxhphoto, pp. 24-25; Seth Perlman/ AP Images, p. 24 (small); Jason Kempin/ Getty Images, pp. 26-27; Carrienelson1, p. 27 (left); Alan Light/ Wikimedia, p. 27 (top); Helga Esteb, p. 27 (bottom); Pakmor, p. 28 (top); Tom Reichner, p. 28 (bottom); Nevodka, p. 29 (left); Elliotte Rusty Harold, p. 29 (right).